For Bames and Stephen

A Thousand Lifetimes

I would wait a thousand lifetimes for you.
Beneath Poseidon's thrashing sea,
to the depths of the darkest, unexplored caves
hiding among the most demonic creatures.
All the while, time would pass like lightning flashes
across ancient meadows; illuminating your silhouette
for only me to see. For no glacier could ever freeze my hand
solid enough that I wouldn't break it, to touch your skin,
knowing that one touch alone would melt it all away anyhow.
I would carry the great pyramids upon my back;
across the burning grains of sand crumbling beneath the weight,
dying of thirst, if only you be the oasis that lie ahead.
If you be a mirage I would drink forever
the taste of Canaan wine from your lips. I would hear the choirs
of angels
harmonize in your voice, and I would float through your eyes
like the mightiest currents of the Nile. I would laugh
as children do; tying together dandelions for a crown,
though they be weeds, they are flowers when placed upon your
hair.
I would stumble through mystical forests, into the witches' den,
to drink whatever potion might turn me to a prince
daring enough to rescue you from the castle tower.
For even a fall, while scaling the walls, would suffice
if only you came in view of the window.
I would scratch and claw back through the seven circles,
to where the cherry blossoms bloom; if only it meant
you might be sleeping beneath the shade.
Covering you with a blanket of lotus petals, so you might never
feel the chill,

only the warmth. I would slip away before you woke,

hoping your dreams told you I was there.

If you be the crime, I'd gladly endure the profoundest damnation.

For even one single moment of true love is enough to carry you

through eternity, and then back again.

Beautiful Winter Green

Did you forget about me?
Everything we had,
and what we used to be?
Texting till we fell asleep
only to wake up to a text that says,
"sorry I fell asleep."
Do you remember laying on my chest
hearing me tell you you're beautiful?
I hope every morning when you wake up,
he tells you too
cause I would if I was there.
If you had morning breath,
I wouldn't care;
I'd still kiss you.
If you left for five minutes,
I'd still miss you. But, I've had years of practice
in letting you go.
I know our ship has sailed,
I just thought I'd let you know;
you're never out of the equation for me.
Explain it to me,
why you can't bring yourself to even say hello?
I see you acting like I'm someone you don't know,
or never loved.
I felt the earth move in bed with you
and I saw the aftermath's tears,
so I know you felt it too.
You remember breaking my heart, right?
That cut deeper than one night ever could,
but you came calling

and there I stood,

night after night.

Then I watched you leave my arms for his.

There was nothing I could do

to convince you of this,

you and me,

everything I wanted since we were thirteen.

Give me one-night present day

cause I still have so much I want to say,

and honestly, I just wanna see your face;

see how you've changed,

and stayed the same.

We can continue this blame game forever,

or you could just remember us as kids

sharing our first kiss

under the ferris wheel.

I never intended to hurt you;

even if that's how it feels.

How could I intentionally hurt someone

I've been in love with since the days of happy meals?

I know we have a lot of history,

but I still believe it's filled with more love

than discontent.

As far back as I can remember

I've been hell bent to be the picture on your night stand.

Please believe me that breaking your heart

was never part of that plan.

Playing it in my mind again and again

won't change the fact

that you're in his bed;

even if you're still in my head.

Firmly planted in my heart.

Two thousand miles apart;

I can't believe I'm feeling this again.
I never knew California
could be cold just like Michigan.

Pillow

Underneath the pillow clouds
of an autumn scene,
sets the fire
raging through my soul.
With no preconceived notion
of which way to go.
Just motion,
and stillness,
in the mind of
a dreamer.
Hoping for a wind
to carry him,
through a journey
meant for storybooks.
Bringing knights to battle
with stunning blades
weighed down by armor
made of chain.
Protecting him
from enemies,
but the only enemy
that kills him,
is the enemy within.
Which is why this creek,
and the water
that rushes over the falls
is the only moment,
that brings him calm.
Before the dawn the yellow turns orange, the red once more.
Lying back against the grass, his hands woven behind his head.
He counts the stars, drawing pictures, telling stories
of fallen heroes.
Once young
and
promising.
Shining like the eyes he used to see through,
but time has made them heavy
among the harsh winters.
Splinters in his hands make them callused,
and worn.
His heart that used to beat true,
now stirs broken,
and
torn.
Then a breeze touches his cheek,

and finds its way through his beard
to find a face still young
and creased
by smile lines
he attempts to hide.
Wondering when nature
will lead him back
to the main
street sign.
Through a Michigan fall
where the leaves change
as quick
as his mind.
But, time moves
to winter.
Where lights cast over the buildings
shine and brighten
the pathway
home.
Even when it's cold,
the love warms his soul.
When the creek water
freezes,
and he steps upon it,
hearing crackling.
Watching spiders spread,
to the corners.
He'll follow the lines
trusting he'll stay above
the freezing water
below,
But perhaps
if he fell through,
tomorrow night
he could use the clouds
as a
pillow.

Hiding amongst the trees

Caring for you
after the storm
resembles many more
magical fantasies
emulating tree trunks
lifting above the roots
lingering below the boots yet
another dream is buried.
Vindicated once again
earthed among the people
newly formed around the bend
twisting through the vines
urged to show true colors
remembering the trap doors
inside the floor boards
never missing a step
imagine the meaning of each breath.
Inviting enemies inside
to see everything you hide
hearing the screams
infest your pride
newly defined breaking divide
kings pushed into the line
in with the rest of the swine
softly changing his walk
to better suit his place
is this what life's like
lying to the master
laying down his soul
laughing among the children
only to realize he's growing old
virtually irrelevant
excelling at the inconsequential
yawning through existence
obsessing over non essentials
umbrellas collapsed once the rain shifted.

Anymore

I'm not sure what to do,
can't you see me gasping for air,
reaching out for you?
Can't you see
the bloodshot in my eyes
from all the
pat them dries,
and smoking fires in the distance,
are you blind?
How could you miss this?
How will you ever fix this?
Give the devil his due,
so he can move on
to his next tricks.
Blowing holes in my heart
the size of Texas,
but I don't hold em
I just let the deck slip,
and splash on the floor,
push in my chips,
sorry guys,
I just don't want to play
anymore.

Do You Have Any Idea How Beautiful You Are?

Do you have any idea how beautiful you are?
I wish you had someone in your life
to remind you some more
when I look at you
I finally understand how Helen of Troy
started a war
and I hate that he didn't make you feel like a queen
when I look at you that's all I can see
behind those eyes
there's a treasure trove of mystery
there's nothing more infinite
than the heart of a girl
and if you'd let me
I'd do everything in my power
to give you the world
I'd dive to the ocean floor
to find you a pearl
and if you need a shore to crash upon
to avoid the rocks
I'll be that for you
if you need a new wind to set your sail to
so you don't wander adrift
I'll be that for you
if you need a fire to warm your soul
before you continue down that road
I'll be that for you
taking the little pieces left of my heart
tossing them in the air
like confetti being swept up after the dance
I guess in the grand scheme
I was never part of your plan
but I hope you think of me somewhere in the future
and the thought makes you smile
I guess we weren't meant to be a forever
we were only meant for a short while
only a moment
if I could control time
I would have slowed it
to see your face some more
or hear you laugh again
I just don't want to imagine your name
coupled with the phrase
I knew her back then
or she's just my friend

it's soul crushing
it's confusing
it's cheek blushing
it's abusing
my heart again
I can't take the feeling of what could have been
one more time
I'm not sure I'd survive
I should be primed
ready for this moment
it's all fleeting
only stolen
like playing chess with your chair on fire
making moves to inch closer to your one desire
who you admire
when the snow falls slowly
through the light streaks
atop mountain peaks
where you feel all the world is right
you feel infinite
if there's a moment with you that exists forever
I'd love to sit in it
skip to it
fast forward to the finish line
where your heart and mine
beat at the same time
either way you've given me inspiration
not that you're just motivation
you've been a total invasion
of my mind
my soul
my heart
when I see you
beats out of control
you're a gravitational pull I can't help but breathe in
you're like a movie I want to watch again
when I know how every scene ends
if you were skipping stones
I'd write my name on all of them
in case there's one you decide to keep
and if you be a dream
I hope I always stay asleep.

Dreams of first loves

What if I called you in thirty years?
Would feelings come rushing back
like a tidal wave of past memories
long forgotten,
brilliantly resurfacing?
Or, would it take you a moment
to recognize the boy's voice
through the sound of the man's?
Would you know
in an instant
who it was
because you'd been waiting
for this moment
for years?
I guess what I'm trying to say
is I know it hasn't nearly been
thirty years,
but I still think about you
in ways I shouldn't. Or in ways
I assumed would eventually
fade away,
but they haven't.
Am I still a recurring character
in your dreams,
as you are in mine?
Or, have the years
slowly made it more difficult
to see me there?

Do you think it's possible
to forget about us
entirely,
even in a hundred years?
Or, do you think even
with a century between us,
you could still find me
buried deep in your memories?
Or, is everything we had
cast to the river of time,
floating out to a sea
overflowing
with the dreams
of first loves?

My Sweet Muse

My sweet muse, who will I abuse from now on?
If I escape through these prison bars,

Will you leave me to tread water all alone?
Will you leave me in the woods, watching me turn stones?
Will you leave me lonely, grasping for air?
Will you keep up the appearance that you're really still there?

Sending up the flair
exploding in the sky,
sending the SOS
falling back down
only to burn my flesh,
but what if I cry?

Will you wrap your arms around me?
Or, would you shoot me in the back as I walked away?

Choke me until my face turns blue,
would you push me off the cliff,
if I asked you to?

Script flipped,
ace on the bottom of the deck,
painting the masterpiece,
missing a speck.
Snapped necks
from the whiplash,
spark the light
of the spliff stash,
until its cashed.
My brains mashed,
but firing on all cylinders,
telling stories to the muses
I've widowed
with my head against their pillows,
trying to fill lows.

Let's just leave for a while,
and come back
after the apocalypse.
When we can scrape the sand,
having missed all of this.

While you walk ahead of me
on the sidewalk,
dragging a piece of chalk,
so I know where to step.
In case I lose sight of you,
wave your hand
on the other side of the sea.
Capturing in a single moment,
eternity.
Can our hearts harmonize
from a distance?
Or, do I need your hand in mine?
If I saw my future without you,
I'd wish to be blind.
If I had two left
I'd twist them
around the vine.
So, I could swing over the water,
but clip it mid-way through,
so I die a martyr,
just in case I couldn't swing
any farther.

Shipwrecks

I haven't stopped loving you for a single second.
I feel like I'm sailing across the sea
in the same boat I wrecked in.
Continuing down the same road;
taking up the torch.
The closer I get to coming to,
the more my mind aborts.
But the thoughts of you still creep in
almost on a daily basis.
Alcohol,
drugs,
and words
are all I have to face this
harsh reality; I've become
what I always feared,
and steered away from,
but I crashed into it.
I was so focused on the rearview,
I missed the exit.
Would you still be there for me
if I said I needed you?
Or, do you see me as someone else,
because of how I treated you?
What if I told you
I miss your sweet smile,
or the way you looked at me
after we talked for a while?
As much as these thoughts
creep in,

they've got nothing
on my demons,
falling off the deep end,
drinking myself to sleep,
having suicidal thoughts
play on repeat.
I'm not the same person I was
when you met me.
Sometimes I think about him, and say,
"who could that be?"
It's just not me anymore.
I've never opened a window,
but damn sure
closed some doors.
Falling backwards
down a wishing well.
Living out of consciousness,
like I fell under a spell,
but there's no healing potion.
I continue moving,
setting myself in motion,
but now I'm swimming in garbage
that's full of ocean.
Trying to act like there's nothing wrong,
hoping no one sees
I'm just a ticking time bomb,
or that I'm fucked up beyond recognition.
The writings written on the wall
like superstition.
People see what they want to see,
which is why I stare through a mirror

hoping to see
who I used to be.
I realize now
dreams have always been fake;
they're thoughts
you don't have the courage
to have
while you're awake.

Window Chairs

If time stood completely still
could we live a moment for a lifetime?
Could we sacrifice growth and pain
for constant laughter and joy?
Would we even need to learn the lessons
life has waiting for us around the next corner?
Could we keep driving with the windows down,
while a song that reminds us of home plays on the radio?
Or, sleep next to the love of our life, never having to worry
about losing the moment to sleep
or losing the moment to the morning sun?
But, pancake batter on my nose and a slow dance in my pajama
pants
awaits me in the kitchen.
If I could spin you around forever I'd die a happy man,
and feel like a kid that never had to leave Neverland.
But, the sadness that follows the movie playing through the
window pane
quickly escapes through the comic strip drawing streaking
through condensation.
A smiley face grins at a wash me on the back of a caravan
traveling to unknown lands, in search of the man
who once promised himself as a boy that he'd climb mountains,
and be a brother to pirates. Photographing jungles,
swinging on vines,
sleeping under the stars and pines,
but the snow shakes off and covers his face.

Who knew a jungle could be so square and cold?

Certainty shakes just as much as the free spirit;

craving some small pieces of this and that,

but never trading this for that.

Being lost on an island gives you plenty of time to stare off into

the sea.

Tell me what it means.

Do you hear the answers?

Or, do you just need the silence?

So Many Things

Every time I see you
I wanna break
but I just let myself bend
because there's so many things
just better left unsaid.

Sometimes it's hard to see the flowers
through all the weeds
so I'll continue to let myself bleed
like I've already bled
because there's so many things
just better left unsaid.

I just don't wanna be part of anymore
of your pain
or confusion
because maybe the story in my head
has all been an illusion
but the movie still plays
of what we could have been
yet still there's so many things
just better left unsaid.

It's not easy to see you
to look into your eyes and know
the next words out of my mouth
will probably be a lie
but just as my heart beats faster
and I'm about to say what's really
running through my head
I say to myself there's so many things
just better left unsaid.

I hear you talking
but I watch you
and think of all the times
I've had dreams of you in my arms
and if I said what I wanted to
would it change everything
or cause nothing but harm
so I let it sit there in my heart
weighing it down
like it's soaked in led
because there's so many things
just better left unsaid.

All the things I wanna tell you
everything I wanna say
but when I hear you talk about him
I'm not sure they would matter anyway
they bubble to the surface
and I continue to refuse
so you'll forever remain
only just a muse
so the words will continue to flame
in my smoke-filled room
while I lie awake in bed knowing
there's so many things
just better left unsaid.

Maybe there's a place
for the future you
and the future me
but before we reach that point
there are still so many moments
we both need to see
so for one last time
I'll eat these words
until I'm full and over-fed
because after all
there's so many things
just better left unsaid.

Untitled (but it's absolutely about you)

Stop, listen for the heartbeat.
Wait a moment for the drop of the sweat beads
stuck in a moment of chance
could it be the same courage to charge into battle
is the same courage needed to ask a girl to dance
or advance through catching feelings
every time you enter the room
my heart starts beating
like you have your own cadence
your presence has its own sound
like I'm patiently lost
not wanting to be found
trying to keep my feet on the ground
drifting toward the sky
I wish I could say it out loud
maybe I'm just too shy
I'm trying not to cry
attempting to stay calm
wondering why or how these feelings came from nowhere
you can find me staring out toward a thought
lost in a blank stare
but daydreams are the only place I can dance with you
or hold you in my arms around a campfire
while you wear my sweatshirt
I'm afraid if I fight for reality we'll both end up hurt
maybe we can flip the script
change the course
finally ride the wave of this invisible force
that's pulling me toward you
I've caught feelings before
but this is something new
like I crossed the street without looking both ways
and got tossed between two trains
when my body floated back down
I landed at your feet
it sounds insane I'll admit that
but from the first moment I saw you
my heart skipped black
and turned red again
everything I wished I said
I'm glad I didn't say it then
I may have missed this moment
may have missed your face
like I'm frozen in time
finally in the right place

trying to keep pace
but my thoughts are moving at light speed
what if you're everything in life I might need
a new seed of planted thought
like I'm swimming as fast as I can to escape
but in your net I get caught
I wouldn't mind in the slightest
if you want to keep me here forever
I won't fight it
for the first time I don't want to run away
you're like the feeling of a summer day
after the harshest of winters
like holding on for dear life
but the wood won't splinter
hopefully it never breaks
we stay awake
fighting off the sleep creeping over the horizon
keep your eyes on me so I can dive in
and heal the broken parts of your soul
I'll do everything I can to help make you feel whole
hear the wind again as it flies through your hair
every moment I've had with you
I wish I was still there
stuck in time
in between dreams
when I'm with you
it doesn't matter what life means
I let go of all the questions
like your putting on a show
and I bought all the tickets in every section
point me in your direction
when I'm lost at sea
if you're looking for a lighthouse in the distance
I pray that it's me
I'll bring you to shore through the storm
if I can
with an army before us all you have to do
reach for my hand
I'll take the burden
take the pain
if you've had one of those days
I'll hold you waiting for the fire to die out in your brain
I'll be your cane, your crutch to lean on
if you feel like falling
I'll be your distraction
if you ever feel like stalling
and you need a laugh instead of a cry
I'd build you a raft to cross the river
so you always stay dry
I'll chase away the monsters from your dreams

I'll hand you the pillow
if you need to muffle your screams
if life feels like it's crashing down
I'll be the one to polish your crown
remind you that you're royalty
of all the words
you're my favorite poetry
maybe you're an answer to the question
of what this all means
because you're a real-life scene
of everything I've ever dreamed.

A Dream of Passion

In a dream of passion you are cast out to sea
and thrashed by the waves
while the monsters gnaw on your flesh
exposing old wounds
creating new scars
creatures surface
in an attempt to lead you to shore
but you stay adrift
drinking the salt water
because your mouth is so dry
the pain you feel
from the hunger
distorts your reality
while vertigo
spins your world
like a top
blinding sun forces you to turn your head
cover your eyes
but your skin blisters
your lips crack
the clouds start to darken
and shift
the waves grow with every passing second
until you are tossed overboard
but you don't swim for shore
or battle the storm
you just float
until the sea swallows you whole
you slowly start to sink
the surface fades

from a sky

to a line

to a dot

 life as you know it takes shape

and forms a million miles under the sea

darkness surrounds you

while your lungs puncture and restrict

but you haven't been breathing all the while

you've been sinking

until your feet hit the ocean floor

lifeless,

cold,

bent,

distorted

your body has been mangled by the darkness,

corrupted by the deep,

imploded by the pressure…

corroded by salt water.

Seashells

I don't know if I can give you seashells
but I can take you to the depths of the sea
below the mightiest reef
down to where the shipwrecks sleep for eternity

I don't know if I can give you seashells
but I can show you the sunrise and the sunset
I can cover you from the waves so you never get wet
I can build you a castle of sand and give you the key
with the power to crush it in your hand if you don't like what you
see

I don't know if I can give you seashells
but I can tell you a story or two
about being lost in an ocean
without a care of being rescued

I don't know if I can give you seashells
but I can give you these arms
and you can wrap yourself in them however you would like
feeling the steady beat of my heart against yours night after night

I don't know if I can give you seashells
but I can give you these words
hoping to enchant you
like the sea does for all of these birds

I don't know if I can give you seashells
but I can try and catch all of your tears before they hit the sand
I can fall asleep to your dreams
holding them safely in my hand

I don't know if I can give you seashells
but I can give you my lips to kiss
and give you the moon for you to eclipse
so you can cut the lights whenever you see sharks
follow me whenever you need to I've learned to see in the dark

If I Could Love You Again

If I could love you again maybe I'd love you differently.
Watch the colors bleed into infinity.
Let the tide wash over me,
drown me,
but breathe in your breath.
If all else fails,
I'll still be obsessed.
Possessed to know you,
one more step to decode you,
one more abyss to float through.
Choke you with my words.
Regurgitating.
Absurd.
Disturbances.
Like the crow on my shoulder,
speaking in tongues,
or the shards of toothpick
swallowed into my lungs.
So I spit up blood
painting my hands red
finger painting my name on your walls.
Trying to pick up all the jacks before the bouncy ball
falls.
Blowing a hole through the floorboards.
Falling through layers.
Screaming on the way down,
but sending up prayers
that hit the ceiling
hovering by the air duct.
Tossed aside like the final
dandelion
plucked.
Weeds are flowers.
Flowers are weeds.
Waiting at the sea of reeds
for miracles we continue to
read.
Leading me to water,
drinking smoke,
reaching a hand out
to hold on to the truth,
or another fire to stoke.
Walk out on the coals
barefoot
arms spread,

face to the sky.
Hoping the raindrops fall
perfectly into my eye.
But, change colors
when they streak
down my cheeks,
or rush over
crumbling mountain peaks.
Time shifting erosion
takes its course,
over the explosion of
remorse.
Regret
shredding the soul in strips
clipped to the clothes line,
letting them drip dry
with the rainbow twine
of a suicide.
Stopped by a messenger,
crushed by those
who pressured her,
or measured her.
Back against the wall,
face on the floor.
Fly away from heaven,
It's only folklore.
Tall tales,
collected in shovel pales,
Tied against the train rails.
screaming for mercy
digging hands into the rusted nails.
Until all of your strength fails,
and you see yourself outside
of your body.
I wonder where my funeral plot
might be?

Snake Eyes

Rolled the dice came up snake eyes
showin two
I've been walking for years
in the same pair of shoes.
Shake em up roll em comin up three
drifting down the riverbank
floating like I'm free.
Throw em again until they flash four
what do I have to lose
it's not like I have possessions anymore.
Toss them out so they roll into five
it's like taking a chance
that you won't feel empty or feel deprived.
Here they go double threes reading that six
puncture wounds through my heart
the bleeding can't be fixed.
Big roll coming up just turned up seven
now I'm rolling up raw papers
closest I'll ever get to heaven.
Change hands not trying to turn up the eight
but the dice read it anyway
can't help but think it's fate.
One more roll then I'm gonna cash out
here it is dice showin nine well I guess now
I gotta keep going
so chop out a line.
I'm gonna toss the next roll fingers crossed they show ten

I need this pot to take myself

places I've never been.

I'm hanging my life on the roll of the dice

so I shake em up twice

throw em on the felt anything but a seven

oh wait that's right time to turn up eleven.

Now we're at our last roll hoping for a twelve

toss the dice they split

and show the double six

so I sit back

and hold up the double fist.

That's it I took the cake

won all I could win

took all I could take

feelin like a mountain

something you can't shake

so I stop by the roulette wheel

put it all on black

spin the ball

watch it bounce back

and slide right into red thirty-three

I lost it all

when I was two steps away

from being completely free.

The Ballad of Stephen and Dooms

The ballad of Stephen and Dooms,
a love story filled with secrets told under the moon
evident by the way energy pours into every room.
Perhaps love stories are always filled
with a level of predestination,
or maybe they are destiny's
greatest manifestation.
Maybe it had been slowly growing
unbeknownst to you,
maybe the love that grows over time,
is the one that blooms most true.
When you find the one you'd scour the universe for
to show them the sun,
after they've been lost in a cold night,
they tend to be the only one
whose head placed on your shoulder
makes the whole world feel right.
Love stories are often times
the most mysterious of tales,
and it may take a few adventures around the world
to find the most beautiful of sails.
Through tell me mores on a distant shore
you felt each other's hearts beat louder than before.
Knowing in a moment,
without yours,
my heart wouldn't be anymore.
At a cliff side,
with a painted scene before your eyes,
your souls wove together
like the mightiest of vines,
and a thought crept into your mind.
"I looked out to the sea,
and looked back to see
a single tear
streak down your cheek,
and I thought to myself,
you're all the heaven I'll ever need."

To Whom It May Concern

I want to break all of the rules with you

I want to run over mountains

and sleep on cliffs

and roll around in throws of passion

barely staying on land

and if we fall

I want to hold you in my arms

and kiss you

the whole way down

hoping our love

will somehow

keep us

airborne

above the ground

and we float through time

like a hover board into the future

where we never grow up

we stay in this illusion of reality

that is so much more fulfilling

never growing old

never dying

never feeling pain

only passion

complete

blinding

passion

for each other

so irrational

so unexplained

that is makes perfect sense

it seems the most

trustworthy moments

in life

are the moments

that have no explanation at all

I want my life

with you

to be just that

I want to explore

and lose ourselves

and find ourselves

in each other

every day.

We're Here

I'm not asking you to speak. I'm not asking you to conjure some
pearl of wisdom from the ancient universe. I'm simply asking you
to be.
For once in our lives.
Look into my eyes when I speak instead of letting them wander
and exist in the fog of potential awkwardness.
Just let go.
It's only the two of us here.
No one will judge you for the intimacy, the vulnerability.
But, my heart is there on the table.
Blood-soaked.
Beating.
For the first time, my eyes are clear enough to reveal it to you.
Please place your hand upon it.
At least show me you aren't as cold as I thought I always had to
be.
We can warm each other, don't you see?
But, all I'm revealing to you now is being received,
like a child telling his father that he'll be an astronaut one day.
When he knows he'd be lucky to be the canary in the coalmine.
Just as quickly as I've begun to build myself up,
not yet with brick,
but with Lincoln logs,
one of the people I'm supposed to trust most
makes me feel smaller still than I ever did before.
So small I feel I could jump on the table,
and hide behind the salt shaker.
Something tells me you would never see me,
you wouldn't even bother to look.
I don't want you to be someone I have to do without,
but I can no longer be around someone who could never look up
to me,
he only looks down.
So, why don't you just shake my hand,
sheepishly toss me a
quiet,
obligatory,
"I love you,"
and be on your way.
I hope we can talk one day,
by the warmth of a fireplace.

Bye Bye Apple Trees

This might be that moment when I realize
I just have to let you go
cause you might not love me anymore
but how can I just walk away from something
my heart has felt for more than half the time
it's even had a beat
it doesn't feel right to accept defeat
when it comes to you
would you still be there for me
if I called
begged
and plead
telling you you're all I need
to keep moving
or breathing
have you come to terms
or are you still seething
tell me when you stopped believing
in us
cause how it all ended still perplexes me
and I still think about having you next to me
it vexes me
it's confusing
all this time were losing
pretending to not still be in love
drinking you away
like I'm alone
in a pub
or a bar

I've had a lot
but you're my deepest scar
one I haven't tried to cover
why is it that I've seen you in every lover
every single moment of intimacy
since you and me
there's one face I see
in case you were wondering
it's you
my only question is
do you see me too
or have I just been a fool
letting my mind wander
taking me places we've never even been
maybe we were
but that was way back when
you looked at me like I was your king
or like you were lost in a dream
whenever I was around
but now my name
is a terrible sound
piercing your ears
but your name has been
my most beautiful sound
for years
rolling off my tongue
I wish I could rewind
to when we were young
and didn't know any better
long before I had enough pain
to write this letter
that paints regret clear as day

line after line
but my intent is to steer you
in the direction that I'm fine
after all this time
even if I'm chasing liquor with wine
to get you off my mind.

Wings

You were given wings to take flight
So that you could fly and taste the sky
Not so you would walk and experience life's plight

You were given wings so you could visit the ancient temples
And feel the weeds overgrown
Letting the wisdom seep into your fingers
Knowing you too could build one of your own

You were given wings so you could feel the warmth of distant
shores
To touch the sands of all the lands
No less, no more.

You were given wings so you could dream
So you could touch the clouds and stars
And circle everything in between

You were given wings because you have a soul
Set on fire from your first breath
So fan the flame so that while you breathe your soul never meets
death

You were given wings to search deep within you
To know yourself above all that seems true
So that when your reflection looks back at you from the sea
You're happy to say, "that's me."

You were given wings so you remember
Even in the dawning age
Birds were always meant to fly
They were never meant to be caged.

Kentucky Slim and The Boys

I went down to Louisiana
met a man with crawfish in his eye
went straight to Alabama
paid for two lovers
then waived em both goodbye
thumbed up to New York
where there's cocaine in the pie
walked straight to LA
hadn't slept in 3 days
went down to Mexico
where you can die a thousand ways
paddled across the sea to Scotland
wept in the highlands
and cried myself anew
drifted to Ireland
and drowned myself
in sorrow and brew
stayed awhile in Iceland
ate quite a bit of sharkskin stew
doubled back to Wales
where I wrote under the milk wood too
met a man from down under
who hit me across the head
with a pint of draft
woke on the Mississippi
floating on a raft
Mark Twain by my side
oh how I cried
and cried

drifted down the stream

carried by the current

this trip ended up being

quite the deterrent

just think of all the ridicule,

the endless jokes

I only left the house

to buy a pack of smokes.

Decided to weave myself a straw hat

and throw on a pair of overalls

got paid to plow the fields

then I trekked over to Chicago

got in a few barroom brawls

needed some more money

so I hustled my way

through a few dozen pool halls

got chased out of town

like a rat with the plague

so I slept on a train

next to a man with one leg

we talked of our lives

and shared stories about our folks

lit up a few joints

and had long drawn tokes

I looked out of the boxcar

at the moon and the stars

thought about how small we are

and wondered if that flicker was Mars

I woke alone

my friend was nowhere in sight

perhaps it was a dream

so I didn't have another lonely night

I traveled the road to Santiago

where I met a gypsy

selling perfume and cologne

worked for him a dollar a day

but that wasn't enough

to pay my way

so I drifted away

and buried my head

in the desert sand

when I was rescued by thieves,

a traveling band,

hauling bags of gold

from the prince's palace

they offered me a drink

from a diamond chalice

I took a gulp

wondering if this was all a mirage

when next I knew

I woke tied to a chair in a garage

apparently due

to unpaid debts

from a series of bets

just think all of this

when I only left the house

for a pack of cigarettes.

Wishing Well Fire

I just fit a square peg in a round hole
saw myself up high
but found myself down low
which means I'm still
under the bed
and by that I mean
I'm deep inside of my head
running through a maze
a place I can stay
and think for days
cause there's so much
to sort through
when I'm screaming as loud as I can
but my volume is on mute
and a brick wall stands in front of me
a hundred feet tall
can't climb it,
go under,
or go through it at all
not sure if I have the strength
feeling like I'm under control
by a monster pulling
the puppet strings
sitting here spinning my wheels
uncertain about what the future brings
if it brings more of this
I'm not sure I wanna move forward with this
maybe I'll rewind

and start walking into my past
but then again
I never wanted that to last
maybe I've always felt like this
maybe I was born like this
but I remember I used to smile
with unclenched fists
when my hair was blonde
since then I've been searching for me
guess I'm not happy with what I've found
I don't dream anymore I just think
I don't see anymore I just blink
I stare into eternity
and wonder if I'm ever gonna see more of me
and if there's more to see
what more I could be
maybe I'm being cynical
even if it feels like I've reached my pinnacle
and hit my head on the ceiling
and moments I'm stealing
from a floating space
a being that's not real
not there
nowhere near
somewhere you can't feel
but you're there none the less
and all your thoughts infest
like termites tearing down a house
or another structure
and every time you see her
it's another puncture
into your heart
and the blood drips out onto your shoe

you try to wipe it off

but there's nothing you can do

it stays there in a puddle

and stays there like a stain

all the effort you made

was all spent in vain

you can try

and try

but you'll run in place

you had your chance

you tripped at the finish line

life smacked you in the face

taught you some lessons

turned you slightly jaded

your mind used to be under your control

until it was invaded

and taken over by the demons

taken over by thoughts

taken over with different meanings

you're no longer the boss

but at what cost

how much do you have left to give

the clock is ticking

not sure you have much time

left to live

might come by your own hand

quick as a thief

it's a common occurrence

when you have no more belief

and life thus far is nothing but dissatisfaction

the wheels are spinning in the mud

and the blood

you have no traction

no way of moving forward
or way of pressing on
the timer just went off
and up in flames goes the bomb
the mushroom cloud covers you
and darkens your lungs
and you have nothing to say
so you trade in your tongue
for another moment
just one more second
to see something beautiful
for one last time
I can't let this be the last image I see
run through my mind
so I cock the gun and get ready
to erase my brain
I'm exhausted from feeling
like I'm going insane
I slide back six feet
after every inch I gain
but no more
I just can't do it
just can't relate
I can't breathe any more
I'm starting to asphyxiate
choking on my own words
but then I free fell under the lotus spell
and I planted flowers inside the wishing well,
they started to grow,
and blistered under the sun,
but there still beautiful enough to show
to anyone.

Cherry Blossoms on the Ground

What makes the cherry blossom beautiful
is not the wonders it bares for the eye to see,
what makes the cherry blossom beautiful,
is that it may not always be.

What makes life worth living
is the very reason your heart's still beating;
the realization that from the moment it begins,
time itself starts fleeting.

Falling off the mountainside is the catalyst for pushing yourself
beyond limitation, to the world of the sublime
which begs the question should every endeavor
(in which you would want to associate meaning) be death
defying?

Potential that we may never speak again
makes it so worth forgiving.
It's a troubling thought that death itself,
is the event that makes life worth living.

Summer Eves

Tell me please
that life will be filled with more
of these summer eves
where infinity is trapped in a bottle
and never leaves
Tell me smiles won't be lost
to the depths of the sea
or hardened still
like the deepest freeze
tell me this suitcase
no longer needs to be packed
for the world and more
I carry upon my back
tell me there's more,
so much more than this
that I'm finally safe
to unclench my fist
breathe in deep your sent
to the bottom of my lungs
desperate underneath the table
hoping to catch crumbs
breaking off of the bread
dripping drops from the wine
swinging through the jungle
getting tangled in the vines
for crimes unearthed
inside the core
like walking down the aisles
and nothing's left in the store

except a section of torn hearts
and greeting cards
because in actuality
we haven't come very far
which is why we still get lost
while gazing at stars
searching for mars
running away from the sound
of screeching cars
honking horns
slamming doors
creating scars
from the thorns of folklore
dancing with myths you seek
but never knew you sought
trying to sneak away
always getting caught
letting grains of sand crack
through the bottom of the hour glass
so time never actually
seems to pass
or pile up at the bottom collecting moments
of thrown fits
and tear drops
how many moments have you wished
time stopped
so you could dance there forever
never enduring the tragedies
when you wake back up
walking home alone
drinking canyon springs
for more life or energy
if your sending prayers

could you say some for me
to the street corner priest
with the letters on backwards
screaming so low
that your voice isn't heard
stealing glances
from a beautiful girl
just for a moment
you don't feel alone in this world.

Crows

Crows bite at my heels,
yet I haven't left the ground
the solitude of nature appeals,
yet I'm too far off to know the sound.
Crunching leaves and back broken sticks
harmonize in my dreams,
but car horns and sirens
blind my vision like high beams.
Frozen in the street
waiting for the death mobile to make a move,
paralyzed with fear
as if standing in front of a nation fully in the nude.
The impact is quick,
yet blunt force
rarely makes the death equally swift.
The pain slowly erodes you
from the inside
like grubs buried beneath the mosaic tree trunk
softened by time.
Oh, death certainly comes there,
evident by the headlight stare,
what may seem like a finger snap's moment
often masks himself as eternities showman.

Turning down Anagrove

I find life an interesting thing.
I think of people that have been in my life
I've watched come and go,
people that have meant the world to me at any given moment,
but now I barely know.
I've shared worlds and universes with friends and family
circled around a campfire, and I've watched them fade away
slowly into the blackness of the night.
I've watched flames rage then watched them tire.
I've felt like a king.
I've felt like a squire.
I've given my heart, and had my heart stolen away.
I've said goodbye to a loved one in front of the gray.
Hearing shots ring in my ears,
watching tears pour down cheeks of those I love,
and hold above all the rest. Which is why I'll never rest
until worry finds a new place to lay.
Where there isn't a single thought left in the minds
of those who have so much to say, but they stay locked away
anyway.
What if memories could save you,
and carry you across desert sands,
until you feel a loved one's hands
saying, "it's my turn to carry your burden;
I can see in your eyes you've been hurting."
Why don't you sit and rest?
Let me tell you a few stories about kings and queens
so you forget about what's been making it seem
like you can't go on. Distorting the colors of the rainbow
twisting your own pot of gold;
sit and rest before your young soul
grows old. Can't you hear the stirring,
and the sweet taste of the morning dew?
Can you feel the same energy I feel too,
left over from the night before?
But, while the morning is still quiet,
let's just sit with each other, and enjoy the silence
without fear of having to speak to fill the air.
It's simply enough to have you near and there.

I love to watch you move, sit, and think.
I could stare at the ones I love
for an eternity. All the while,
wishing I never had to blink.
I've laughed until I cried
because of laughter alone, not knowing or caring
why we were laughing at all.
I've felt the presence of an army behind me,
even with my back against the wall.
I suppose gratitude would be in order
for the cards I've been dealt,
but gratitude is nowhere near a strong enough word
to express the love that I've felt.
I can remember so many moments
when I've looked up and seen a familiar face,
and in a million years,
it's a face I would never replace.
I've seen hearts shattered, and tossed,
and I've seen those very hearts
put back together over a pot of pasta sauce.
What an amazing feeling to feel
that there's nowhere on earth I'd rather be,
and there's no group of people
I'd rather see. If I could travel back through time
to be with you again,
in an unforgettable moment,
I feel as though I'd be walking forever.
So, for now, I'll sit and dream of the next time
we will all be together.

Standing at the Counter

If we would have crossed paths when our dreams were aligned,
do you think everything at this moment would be fine?
Do you think we'd still be crying?
Dying a little inside with every breath,
hoping you'd be around the corner with every step?

The House Painter's Tale

Hello, I'm a house painter. Have you painted many houses, well no, but I have painted many doors. Terrific, are you good? Oh yes sir. I believe my brush strokes strike even, true, and beautifully. My attention to detail is astounding, I rarely leave a single spot uncovered, and if I do, I cover it quickly blending it back together with the original composition. Do you love house painting? Oh yes, sir. I love it more than anything. I love the fresh smell of the paint poured into a tray, I love the softness of the clean brush bristles against the back of my hand, but most of all I love taking that which was barren, or merely a shell and giving it such life to it that the passerby might utter, "Wow, how beautiful." It's the only passion I've ever known, sir. I admire your heart's desire; however, I have no painting positions for you today. Come back after some time. Yes, sir. I will come back.

Sir, hello, have you any house painting positions available, I've waited for months now. Have you been spending your time wisely? Well, yes sir, I've visited many new places, and I've met many new friends. I am quite enjoying my time here. That is all well, and good, but what of your painting, have you been practicing? Well, no sir, you told me to wait and come back for a job after some time. Oh, I see, well son, unfortunately no job, once again. Come back after some time. Yes, sir.

Hello sir, have you any house painting positions? I've waited for months and months now. Have you been spending your time wisely? Well, sir I'm beginning to grow restless, and tired. The initial thrill of this new place has sense faded, and now much of what I know seems routine, as if I'm walking through the pages of my own storybook with my eyes closed expecting to be able to tell the story afterward. Oh, I see, and what about your painting, have you been practicing? Well, no sir, again you told me to wait, and come back to you after some time. Oh, I see, tell me, how do you feel of your own painting ability? I still feel I could be a good house painter sir, I mean maybe not as good as some, but perhaps with some consistent work I could become better. I'm not sure, sir, I'm not sure. Oh, I see, I've seen this corner your heart is bending around many a time; however, I have no painting positions for you today, come back after some time. Yes sir, I will.

Hello sir, I know it's been quite long, but have you any house painting positions available? I've waited for an eternity now. Have you been spending your time wisely? Well sir, I've tried to make the best of my time, but I feel as though I've been sailing across the pacific with neither a sail or a compass, barely even being thrown about by the wind. Oh, I see, and what of your painting, your most burning desire, have you been practicing? Oh, well no sir. You see you've told me to wait so long that I haven't felt the feeling of a brush in my hand for what feels like forever. I haven't smelled the fresh paint of a can newly opened, I haven't felt the dry brush bristles against the back of my hand, I haven't seen the dull become beautiful in so long. Oh, I see, well son, I have no new house painting positions for you, come back after some time. Sir, I'm not sure in my heart of hearts I will be back, perhaps I will someday, but before I go. Who is the young man over there? The one painting the side of the house facing east? Oh, that young man is the new member of the house painting crew. Sir, I beg your pardon, but I've come to you time and time again wondering if you had any available positions and you turned me away again and again. Why did this young man gain the position that should have been mine? Oh, I see, well son like you, he was an eager young painter whose only burning desire was to be a house painter, so after I denied him the first time, he went home and painted his own house.

8 Days from Now

I guess I have to scream it
is that what you're saying
cause I've tried everything
from writing to praying
and playing pretend
I've never had any interest
in you being my friend
but where you living these days
cause I have about a thousand letters to send
about how I've thought about you every day since you were mine
it's like divine intervention
it has to be
cause I swear every other line I mention you
and what you meant to me
what you still mean
since the days of winter green
and children's dreams
making you jealous
cause even if you were hating me
you were still thinking of me
and now I'm blinking to see the past
cause I'm scared of sinking into the future
without you
what if I let the storybook
love of my life
slip right through my fingers
as much as I try and shake it
that thought still lingers
it's haunting

but of all things it's disheartening

cause I've just been chasing the feeling I always got from you

but I guess I wouldn't know what love is

if not for you

I just don't know what to do to make you see

that I think you were meant for me

and I was meant for you

but I've known that from the first moment I saw you

so this is nothing new

but it's all true

I couldn't fabricate that

I'd love to elaborate in fact

cause how would you explain all of this

how could I possibly be that amiss

about this situation

but that's exactly what causes all this frustration

it's like looking at the constellations

they are

always have been

and always will be

just like my love for you

and your love for me

but you insist on denying

that I wasn't trying

to hurt you

but stop and think

really think about that for a minute

cause cloud nine isn't nearly incredible enough

to describe what that night was to me

I think I'm still lost in it

or in our first kiss with everyone watching

I was so nervous

but the lights faded away

the sounds went silent

you were wearing a denim jacket

you looked so stylish

but you could have worn anything

it really didn't matter to me

you've always been beautiful as can be

I've always felt you were a little out of my league

but I still feel you're exactly what I need

cause you feed my soul

and fill my pages

you always did

and probably will for ages

cause I don't know that I see you in my arms ever again

if I had a crystal ball

I wouldn't have let you go back then

but for now

I'll just keep moving this pen

and wonder when if ever

you'll be mine again

like you've always been

but for now

I'll just remember

sitting here

waiting for December.

Winter Drowning

I wish I could fly south for the winter.

Spread my wings, and let the cold air lift me high into the sky

until I pass out from the lack of oxygen.

Then I'll wake up in the ocean,

but I won't drown I'll just sink and sink

into a shipwrecked vessel

filled with treasure undiscovered,

and bathe in the gold coins and precious gems.

Wading through the water like a sandstorm in the desert.

I wish I could dive deep into the sea,

but the water wouldn't grow darker the further I descended

it would brighten and brighten

like a supernova,

or a single, desperate church candle.

I wish I had legs to carry me through the winter,

and above the heavy clouds looming.

Not wings, but legs so I could run above the clouds.

Keep running never turning around to see them fall,

and evaporate on the concrete.

Oh, how the precipitation changes

from season to season,

but the winter's is heavy and so very cold.

Boxcar Dreams

Off I go off I grow to sell my soul

$50?

How about $25 and a pack of smokes

and a tattoo of a devil on my shoulder telling jokes

hoppin on a southbound train

listen to the gears turn until I go insane

rise from the ashes and roar like a lion with a stifling full main

sleep in a few rice paddies and pay my way

picking every single little grain

but as I look to the western sea board

I pray but I don't talk to the lord

Tuphos

I saw a couple ladies cryin,
lookin for a muse of fire when,
they took me through a walk in the Nile, and
said these are tears we dive in.

Saw a couple people smilin,
lookin for vices to die in,
wonder how far we can float,
before we start capsizin.

Read a couple books that told me,
My life's just a mystery,
read a couple newspaper trimmings,
about the good days were missing.

I wonder if everyone knows what,
old Billy tried to show us,
that's there's always been hurricane floods,
and there's always been insane love.

Throw on the record and dance,
forget about all your plans,
breathe in a loved one or two,
turn off the evening news.

Saw a couple reaching hands for,
a life filled of wish we had more,
saw a couple children playin,
in sand castles maybe worth savin.

Heard a couple poets dancin,
words into sweet romance, and
saw a couple princes prayin,
for towers and dragons worth slayin.

Life isn't quite what it seems,
sometimes it's smoke and it's dreams,
might as well cast out the lines,
swim till you swallow the tide.

Darker Days

I've been crushed by a wave that was tidal
crazy thoughts spinning through my head
borderline suicidal
but it's round three
and I'm back again
Demons circling around me
and I'm about to bend
but I ain't about to break
I'm swinging back for my own sake
strap in with no hands
whatever it will take
to pull myself out
pull myself through
round two
took one on the chin
thought I was moving up
thought I was about to win
but I got put down right on the canvass
I saw it going differently in my mind
I never would have planned this
but it happened
and I can't go back in time
still fighting for my life
trying to get mine
I ain't gonna let this keep me from my destiny
I got lots to give
still haven't seen the best of me
or the rest of me
I'm not checking out
I'm not throwing in the towel
even if it's foul
even if it starts to stink
and I start to sink
and the water closes over my head
I'll do my best to breathe
and my best to believe
I can keep floating
until I start swimming
until I start paddling

even if the thoughts in my mind keep rattling
I'll keep battling
cause I'm stronger than this
I was born to be more
even if the journey wounds me a few times
and my body is sore
and this thing weighs me down
and I'm the only one around
I'll wake up again
I can see the sun slowly creepin in
it's starting to look brighter
I can see the path once more
it's a little more uphill
then it seemed to be before
but I take the first step
left after right
I just laced up my gloves
ready for the fight
with a wounded wing
wounded heart
wounded soul
but I ain't knocked down yet
I have to sing
have to start like a stone
roll like a cart
close to the vest
I can feel it coming
literally feel it in my chest
today might be darker
I might feel a little heavy
but I'll never let it break me
like a hurricane does a levy
I'm still standing tall
well maybe a little hunched over
but I'm trying to clear
some of this weight off my shoulder
trying to clean myself up
and get back on the right path
I've been down a different road lately
a little rough patch
but I'm used to it by now
sometimes I feel like the sun is shining
but it's buried by the clouds

but I know it's still gonna rise
and to my surprise
it's another new day
that I've opened up my eyes
and I'm starting to see
all of this beauty that's surrounding me
I'm not looking down on me
I'm tryin to stay above me
cause I know I have more people than most
that love me
but sometimes it's hard to feel it
there are moments in my life
that I want to peel it
and step out of my skin
and grow a new shell to hide under
cause it rains in my head
and I hide from the thunder
I hurt the ones I love
cause I stay away and hide alone
won't even say hello
when they call on the phone
but it's got nothing to do with you
please try and understand
the only thing that would make me feel better
is holding your hand
but I'm not there right now
I'm in a different place
I'm being pulled down by the chains
of my own head space
and the sight of my own face
but please believe me when I say
I'm doing all I can
I'm trying to pick myself up
but I'm only just a man
but I can feel the wind again
it just changed direction
I'm getting off this highway
at the next intersection
I'm gonna drive for miles
into the horizon
no more thinking
no more sinking
I'm sick of fuckin capsizing

I'm coming back to the surface
coming back with a purpose
and one things for certain
if it comes around again
at the end
I'll still be standing.

To Whom It May Concern Too

73

I wanna drive across the country

with no destination in sight

just drive and drive

until day becomes night

sleep in a boxcar

with a cigar as my only light

pick a guitar

to keep me company

chop a line

let the rush feel me

nothing to dream of

but my thoughts and fears

nothing to drink

but my loneliness and tears

I'll stop off in the wild west

sit for a while in a saloon

drink and drink

let my head swell like a balloon

until it pops

and my body drops

to the floor

or a bottle breaks over my back

then I'll hop back on the train

and take it all the way down the track

Empty Wind

Let me suffer through an empty wind,
and stockpile all my sin.
Let it drop through an hourglass.
It seems I lived this life before, a little too fast.

Let me break and build myself up again.
Let the tide cascade over my head.
I wanna see if I'm strong enough…
I wanna see if I'm strong enough.

I remember being young with you.
I remember doing drugs with you.
Floating through universes, somewhere in the sea,
watching the sun set from a blanket on the beach.
I swear I could get lost in this moment, for the next generation to
see.
And, while you looked out, I looked at you; you didn't notice.
I miss the moments that words don't even do justice.

Let me learn and fail in my own way.
Let the tears carry me to a new place.
I wanna see if I'm young enough…
I wanna see if I'm young enough.

Let's get lifted, and dive deep into a conversation
we only have when we're this high above the ground.
Let's have a few drinks,
go back to your room, and maybe fool around.

Let me scream to my own tune.
Let me harmonize in a cold room.
I wanna know if I've loved enough…
I wanna know if I've loved enough.

End of the Aisle

If I could have that night back,
I swear I'd do things differently.
I'd tell you how this is everything I've ever wanted,
how I always intended it to be,
how I pictured this moment for years;
between heartbreaks and long nights
from fighting back tears
and making songs write
away my thoughts of you.
I never thought when the moment finally came
I wouldn't have the words to say.
So, I'll let you walk down the aisle;
if you can say with the utmost honesty
that it's him you dream about at night,
and it's no longer me you see.
But, if there's a single shred of doubt,
then let me have that conversation back.
Let me make up for the chance I missed;
with a chance to convince you
that I've been the one for you since your first kiss,
to our first school dance.
From pictures in our lockers,
to phone calls for hours,
from trading punches like boxers,
and being yours,
but now hers.
It just doesn't feel right to not have you next to me;
it doesn't feel real.
I mean, wasn't I just trying to make you jealous
by taking another girl on the Ferris wheel?
But, if you're truly happy with him
then I'll keep trying to let you go,
but if there's any doubt at all
all you have to do is let me know.
I'll be on the next plane leaving LA.
I'll be back in Michigan today.
I'll sprint through the airport
like they do in the movies;
I'll pick you up in my arms
and spin you around till we're dizzy.
I'll kiss you like I did at the fair
when we were just kids
because all I wanted then
and all I want now
is this.

So, don't dismiss the possibility
that it was always supposed to be you and me.
Loving each other through the deepest depths of infinity.
Because I prayed for you when I was young,
and now all I can say to you is I was young,
when I did what I did
if I could have another go around as a man
not a kid,
I wouldn't mess it up again.
I'm a different person now
than I was back then.
So, when you're dressed in white,
and it's not me at the end of the aisle;
I hope you know I'm drinking you away tonight…
the same way I have been for a while.

Madman

The steampunk rolling vision of a sideways dream
perplexes even the shadowless wolves
near the fireside
and drowns the carpet stain into the dew fall
where it is soaked between leaves
falling through dimensions of time
twisting upon the back of a brick paver pallet
that protrudes around the street corner
with a man pointing and saying,
"I've been here on this same spot for two tenths of a decade."
Or so he may figure
but becomes disfigured by life itself
behind the wondering child rolling down a hill
galloping through the wind-soaked forest
dreaming of some giant crushing grapes in his hand
and drinking the juice that falls and ferments from his palm
but all of the sudden the screams of a madman
flood through the walls
of a modern hillside mansion
burning to ashes
but the child draws a sketch with his finger
of a stick figure family
weeping and wondering
chills of an aching back creep across the plains
diving through canyons
spilling blood lust of ancient villages
or crusading Templars across a field of sorrow
spoken among whispers,
secrets creeping through time
short of a time capsule
spinning around in circles attributing memories
to a day trip through southern colonies
forward to a revolution cry
truth carriers among widows and soldiers perched upon window
sills
swinging their legs
talking of fairy tales while locked in dungeons
sprinkled throughout lands and tears trickling
but gathering in puddles turned red by sulphuric rock
"I've seen it twice!" Cries the crow
but bewildered he is as he flaps and dives
worms crawling through grass wet with warmth
cut between seven hearts all beating differently

flowing among precious gems
but forever buried
what a waste to have such beauty only seen by centipedes
because even a hundred legs
couldn't carry a man through the twists and turns of life
and the sudden shock and shell of twice turned memories
fading into abyss,
"I wonder if Blackbeard ever cried?" Asks the man
while rogue waves overwhelm his ship
capsizing it to the deep to join the rest of the lost corsairs
foolhardy rushing against tides
trapped between lockers and stones
tossed between dreams
swords and flintlocks that are left behind
not brought through the crowded city streets
floundering under the pressure to perform
build and rebuild passion pillars
crumbling like the ancient temple of Zeus
only a shell of his former self oh but what he stood for and what
he was
can only be remembered through scribes and spoken stories
changed and changed again from ear to ear
I've told you now and again
I suppose tribes can remain among civilization
but the overwhelming numbers might consume integrity
eventually
unannounced but ever present
always ticking and ticking
like the clockwork of the inventor of time,
"have you seen his workshop?"
The old man asked me while lighting his cigarette
with a broken match
but luckily the brick stroke
sparked just enough for a flame
that dwindled of course eventually disappearing
to a growing string of smoke
waving with the wind and fading...
oh how it fades
whistling silently
but spectacular
sparking only madness in the mind of the
sane man
and only sanity in the mind of a
madman.

Years and Miles

If we could bundle together all of the words
we said or didn't say
and send them far away
do you think they'd find their way
into another fairytale
or someone else's love story
cause we aren't getting much use
out of the phrases these days
or the moments lost in a haze
like we're the only two people that exist
but I see a lot more people around me these days
I must admit it feels like I don't fit
here or there or anywhere
since I rolled out of your arms
and you slow danced into my dreams
cause that's the only place I'm still with you
the only place I still smell your hair
after you jump in my arms to say hello
like you haven't seen me in years
when we saw each other five minutes ago
the only place I can sing to you
until you fall asleep on my chest
and my arm falls asleep under your neck
but I'd rather the bone break through
than move and wake you
the only place we can argue
until the tears well up
and the shots are taken then developed

realizing we wouldn't be crying if we never felt loved,

the only place I can still see you again for the first time

play it back, watch it again

then rewind I dare you to define

what we're feeling, what we felt from the start

still in love after years and miles apart.

Song of a Flower pt.3

It's about that time of day
when I try and drink you away
and think off all the things
you wouldn't let me say.
So, I'm sitting here wondering
what would have happened that night,
with a bottle of wine and some feelings?
I was at the same table at dinner;
I saw the looks you were stealing.
I felt you wanting to stay in the car.
I could literally feel the hesitation
watching you reach for the door,
could you hear me hitting the steering wheel
out of pure frustration?
Did you see me sink into my seat,
completely defeated?
I wasn't sure if I told you I loved you,
that you would even believe it.
All I needed was one more moment
alone with you
then I could have shown you in person
all of these feelings
I've kept buried.
Maybe you had a feeling
of what I would have said,
so, I guess I'll send you a gift
once I hear you got married.
Do you ever find yourself wondering
what I would have said?
I still find myself wondering
if you think of me late at night
lying in bed.
Hey, remember the first time we talked
in that living room?
I remember the way you looked at me,
and made me feel like a king with a smile.
Or when we used to rehearse
just the two of us?
Using it as an excuse
to spend more time together.
We used to laugh and play;
you made me feel happy like a child.

I could have rehearsed that play every day,
and performed it forever.

We didn't need an audience.
We didn't need a script.
Everything that happened on stage
was true love in motion,
especially when we kissed.
I can still feel your lips,
and remember how I used to drop lines on purpose
so we had to run the scene again,
and kiss for far too long.
Then I'd stumble over the next few words
because it was real for me.
I wasn't acting.
I didn't realize when you fall in love,
you can actually feel your chest contracting.

Kentucky Slim and The Boys Pt. 2

I'll tell you a story I stumbled upon
while on a drive
about the man
who taught me how to live
and live while I'm alive.
I wandered off the interstate,
off of 75, and I walked right into
a beat up old dive.
I peeked my head in
and took a seat at the first open stool
while the man across from me
lay asleep in a puddle of his own drool.
I pulled out my smokes
and put them atop the bar
as the keep motion to me
and asked me what I'll have
in a thick Irish brogue
it had been a while since I'd come in
so I scanned the bar
then ordered a stiff glass of gin.
I looked in the corner
after some loud noise
and some a group of men,
perhaps they were boys.
But the man that sat in the middle of the pack
oh, you could tell it was him,
and that was first when I laid eyes on Kentucky Slim.

"Mama kicked me out when I was 17 years old
then I had to sleep
on the street in the blistering cold
I had to stand by a fire
until my hands were scolding
then I started packing coke in my coat
they call that holding
I worked on steamboats
and robbed banks like the wild West
locked hands and squared up with Jesse James
slept with a 45 on my chest
that's when I walked through the Smokey's
and watched the sun set
and won half a million
on a chance and a bet
turned around with a woman
and spent together a long night
woke in the morning
and my wallet felt a little lite
she took everything
nothing for me to retrieve
but after all I wasn't paying her to stay
I was paying her to leave.
I hustled my way across the states
hopping from bar to bar
I got locked up for grand theft
after getting caught stealing car after car.
Did hard time twice
at good ole Folsom
the fellas there were
witty, hardy, and wholesome.
Traveled some miles

and sat on the edge of a few river banks
I would look up at the sky often, smile,
and think about giving thanks
then I would smoke a little smoke
and have an occasional toke
with the lonely traveler
and for the night we would be the best of friends
until the next day
when we would send each other on our way.
It seems I've been around the world
a thousand times,
lay in a million beds
and loved the best I could
but I never stayed around
until the next morning
I guess the way you should.
I would move from night to night
and day to day
only stopping for
a drink,
a bump,
a dream,
a chance,
a song,
a life,
a love,
a dance.
When you live
like the night will never end
you can live a lifetime
in just a few hours
you can learn all there is about a person
you can build castles,

you can build towers.
When you love,
if only for a moment,
like you've never loved before
and never will again
you can circle around the world twice
and see things anew
like you've never been.
Anyway,
I would wander wherever the wind took me
wherever my feet hit the road
it never intrigued me to settle down
and build a humble abode.
I remember one pool hall
to be specific
oh the scenery how it changed
the atmosphere was terrific.
There were brawls in the corner
and sex on the stairs
there were broken windows
and only three or four chairs.
Everyone there was tough
and knuckled up at one wrong glance
you better be ready for a hell of a night
you better wear your drinking pants.
Hard whiskey,
that's what we drank
with an occasional line
I see you are drinking gin there
I never liked the smell of pine.
Ah, but the smell of a Georgia pine,
just after the winter,
now that will make you smile

now I need to stop
and just think of that for a short while."
"How did you get the name Kentucky Slim?" I just had to say.
"Ah that's a story for a different time, a different day."
Anyway, that's the story of Kentucky Slim
maybe you know him?
Maybe you don't?
Maybe you'll meet him,
maybe you won't...
perhaps you already have met him
and you have to remember and see,
perhaps he lives inside of you,
perhaps he lives inside of me.

I'll Just

I'll just stick to dreams about you.

I'll just stick to words about you.

I'll just sit and wonder if you're ever coming back to me.

I'll just try and stop thinking about you.

I'll just tell my friends you're some girl.

I'll just flip through the pictures.

I'll just replay everything.

I'll just keep loving you.

I'll just…

Lights on

I'm kneeling
staring down the barrel of a 12 gage
and I'm standing in front of an empty crowd
an empty stage
reading from a notebook
with an empty page
there's no one listening
and the lights are shining
so my sweat is glistening
my heart is pounding
beating out of my chest
and I think about you daily
keep you close to my vest
passing the test
but failing on the book report
and I'm stranded on an island
not a packed resort
drinking champagne
I've got a bucket outside the door
catching the rain
so I can quench my thirst
pull the trigger
catch a ride in the hearse
snatch a purse
so I can grab a bite to eat
don't tell on me
keep me discreet
a secret
whisper in your ear

give you the route

tell you where to steer

and where to veer

drive off the road into the canyon

plain and simple

drawn like a crayon son

like a burnt sun

or a sun burn

sit back

and watch the world turn

watch the seasons change

still the same

still just as strange

as when I was a boy

all alone

sitting

shaking

waiting for my mom

to come home

making chicken nuggets

and mozzarella sticks

building houses

with tooth picks

to pass the time

watching Michael Jackson videos

do you remember the time

black or white

it's dark outside

alone again tonight

fall asleep on the couch

with all the lights on

so it never gets dark

if someone comes to the door

the dog will bark
scare them away
man of the house
turned 12 years old today
learned how to shave from a TV show
no dad around
mom where'd he go
mind of a madman
mind of a sad man
nightmares of the sandman
waking up screaming
can't distinguish reality or dreaming
creating my own world
trying to scrape up diamonds and pearls from the dirt
clothes dirty wearing the same shirt two days in a row
chronicles of a boy
raised by a single mother
and a boy learning to be a man
from his older brother
found love from the neighborhood kids
our own little crew
used to steal candy at the Sunoco
Charleston chew
bag of skittles
started writing at 12
rhymes and riddles
stone face showing no elation
sleep in the back of class
give a damn about my education
teaching myself
I'm the professor
notebook in my backpack
I confess to her

tell her my secrets all my fears

let her feel my heart catch my tears

wrinkled dots on the page cause a blemish

can't lie to you can't embellish

but I'm deep in thought so I relish the idea of growing up

it's a fetish the idea of blowing up

sewing up the cuts

and breaking the stitches

growing up collecting quarters for a grilled cheese

no riches

bowl of tomato soup cold out the fridge

climbing back in bed

building dreams like a bridge

carry me across the water

part the sea

keep searching

looking deep

king inside of me

maybe if I keep my hands tight so my knuckles stay white

I can aid in avoiding another Friday night fight

if heaven was around the corner

I'd turn and walk the other way

what more do I have to say

lost my faith

all my life had holy water

shoved in my face

but I run in place

and spin my wheels

leaning back

staying on my heels

speaking truth

expressing real feels

heart on my sleeve

about to leave

late to the checkout

paid for the room twice

buried deep being searched for

like head lice

or raw rice

cracking my tooth

split

rude

uncouth

soothsayer guitar riff

back stiff like a statue

standing upright

let your hair down

why so uptight

take it easy

if you miss me open my pages

so you can see me

look at my body

so you can read me

this is where I live

this is my home

the only thing that makes me feel alive

not alone

I got the world at the end of my pen

maybe the world will read it

just don't know when

but I can send prayers to heaven

till I die at twenty-seven

like Jimi

all I ask for is all the love you can give me

show me the universe

bring me the sun

tell me you'll stay

and be my only one

where'd you go

can't see you through the dark

peeling off my skin like tree bark

deep roots

gripping the soil

down through earths layers

and I feel like a number

coming out on conveyers

with a barcode stamped on my neck

one drink too many

fell off the back deck

split my head

brain fell out

rolled away through the yard

no more thoughts to write

like an old bard

shuffle the cards

deal me the ace of spades

angry about all the times I prayed

no one spoke back

chest twisted

like I'm having a heart attack

cardiac arrest

forgot to take a breath

two lines away from meeting death

what could my next thought be

chronicles of being raised by a single mother

and what it taught me.

Spring and Fall

What if we went away to a place that always felt like springtime,
or a place where a Michigan fall played on repeat
like a public service announcement?
Every morning we could watch the leaves change;
instead of television, we could read Emerson, Whitman, and
Frost
to give our eyes a break from the light. We could listen
to the pages scrape one another as they turn,
needles scratching records as they spin,
and my hand in yours
as we dance on the porch that wraps around our front yard.
We could walk through the garden
playing mini games of hide and seek.
Until I pick a rose,
and put it to my nose,
then hold it out for you to keep.
What if fall lingered, and never became winter,
but spring sprung when we wanted it to?
There would never be a summer, never a winter,
just spring and fall. Because after all,
we grow and fall,
grow and fall. Then grow again
leaving the winters and summers behind
to chase peace with a friend.

Time

I've been walking for a thousand years

I've run ten thousand days

I've seen the leaves change 100 million ways

now I've seen the moon rise all across the land

I've seen the sun set in the palm of my hand

I've wished time would fly away

and I've begged god for just one more day

oh it's time we wish away

and it's time we beg for on our final day

Now I've collected my rage

in an hour glass

I've sat and watched the sand

slowly drop past

I've daydreamed for hours

in the back of a room

hoping I would reach my dreams

oh so soon

I've let new people

just slide on by

I've never stopped to ask myself

why

oh it's time we wish away

and it's time we beg for on our final day

Moments flash like a bolt of lightning

across the sky

you'll pass someone you once knew

and you won't even stop

to say hi

time will twist you

flip and change your mind

you'll find things you once loved

you've left far behind

you'll drive yourself mad

with the dreams you've been chasing

and you'll contemplate often

the time you've been wasting

oh it's time we wish away

and it's time we beg for on our final day

When that day comes

and god closes your final door

you'll see your reflection one last time

wondering if you could have been more

or you'll welcome the end

with a whimper or a sigh

but when all is said and done

you'll finally kiss the sky

oh it's time we wish away

and it's time we beg for on our final day.

Song of a Flower pt. 2

I'm staying awake

just so I can think about you some more,

but who am I kidding?

The second I fall asleep

I'll dream of you.

What kills me the most?

I know you feel the same way.

Are you keeping yourself

from reaching for the phone too?

Tell me what I should do.

Do I fight for you,

and lay it all on the line?

Should I be brutally honest,

and tell you how my chest physically hurts

when I think about the fact

that you are with someone else.

Should I tell you that I think about you constantly?

Should I tell you about how many times a day

I reach for the phone

to tell you something funny,

but I put it back down?

Should I just tell you that I love you,

and I want to be with you?

I've wished I was with you

ever since the first time I saw you.

Should I tell you about how I've written a million words about

you?

The salt in the wound?

You are probably in his arms as I write another line about you.

Can you hear me thinking about you?

I swear sometimes I can feel it;

I can feel you thinking of me as I think of you.

I know you don't want to hurt him,

and I don't want you to

but I'm hurt every second I have to breathe without you.

I'm hurt every moment I can't share with you.

I'm hurt every time I've wished I could call you.

I'm hurt every time I think about what we could have been.

I'm hurt thinking of every time I've seen you cry,

and I knew it was because of me.

Why doesn't life have a fucking rewind button?

Why do you learn the lessons

when it's too goddamn late to do anything about it?

Can't we flash forward to get a little glimpse,

just to see what path we should take?

I just don't understand

why love has to be so complicated

because knowing what I know now

it's not complicated at all.

In fact, it's as simple as one plus one.

I love you,

and I want you

and only you,

each and every day

from here on out.

I want to share those moments with you.

I'm sick of putting the fucking phone down.

I'm sick of staying up thinking about you and him.

I'm sick of holding you in my dreams.

I'm waking up and walking out into reality.

You are supposed to be with me,

can't you see that?

There's no way you don't feel it when we see each other.

Let's just run away together.

Let's get in the car

and leave everything and everyone

so far behind

we forget where we came from.

Promise me one thing:

promise me you'll never forget

how I made you feel.

I'm going to run away,

and of all people you know where I'll be.

So, I'll look for you morning after morning,

and if you decide never to come

I'll understand.

After all, I've gotten used to loving you in my dreams.

Goodnight.

Tell him to give you a kiss for me.

On the Sidewalk in Hell's Kitchen

I walk the line,
then I chop it up and snort it,
cocaine blues
cause I can't even afford it.

Struggling to stay true,
chasing my dream of passion,
I'm down to my last crust of bread
all I have left of my ration.

My shoes have holes in them,
my jeans are ripped,
my heads about to explode
because the wires been tripped.

I saw a man with white around his eyes
wearing a black apron
scraping paint off the wall
and eating the chips
maybe to get high
he looked like he had a hell of a life
and maybe not much left to give
then he let out a sigh to suggest
he couldn't believe this was the life he lived.

21st century screams.
First world problems;
while a refugee nurses her baby

on the streets where a mob looms.
She wipes her tears
and rocks her baby while it cries;
while a 19-year-old American boy cries
that he can't get a burger and fries.

Step back.
Think.
Have a little perspective.
You don't have to be a private investigator
or a detective,
to see the truth,
see what's really going on.

A little African boy,
with diamonds under his finger nails,
chop off his hand
and sell the whole thing at Zales.
Let me clip the finger nails
so the rock can really shine;
walk down the aisle
and let the wedding bells chime.

A little Syrian girl is swooped
and sold in a sex trade by a radical group;
while an American girl throws a fit on her birthday
cause she only got white gold hoops.

What are we saying?
What message are we spreading?
Another refugee prays to God that he can just hold on
and keep treading
maybe make it to shore
only to get shipped back
and get beheaded in the street.

Where does the buck stop?
Who answers the call?
Does it depend on one of us,
or does it depend on us all?
I'm not trying to make noise or be a hypocrite
all I'm saying is have more perspective,
and empathy,
and maybe,
just maybe
love more… at least a little bit.

Behind Every Door

Would it be alright to say
I hope you walk through every single door
I sit behind?

That way I could finally confess
all of the thoughts I have
stored in the corner of
my mind.

If you saw me sitting at the far table,
would you say hello,
just to be nice?

Or would a weak smile,
and a forced wave,
suffice?

I would hope
you come sit with me.
Pour yourself some tea,
and tell me what you're thinking,
so it doesn't remain a mystery.

Would you find it confusing
to see me again?
Or would you find comfort,
in the eyes of a friend?

If I reached for your hand,
would you watch me take it?
Would seeing it remind you
of your heart, I once held,
when you watched me break it?

Do you think love
every really fades?
Is anger just a convenient disguise
for pain?

Do I still seem the same
as I was back then?
I'm not sure what's harder to bare,
what is,
or what could have been?

If you walked in
what's the first thing
you'd say?

Because I wouldn't know.

Just promise
that if you walk in today,
you'll at least come over,
and say hello.

Cliff's Edge

What happens to a singer that no longer has the voice to sing?
What happens to the dancer who no longer feels the rhythm in
his body?
Can you explain the loss of inspiration?
How can you explain when a poet runs out of words?
A poet sits alone on a Greek island staring out into the Aegean
Sea
watching the sun quite literally, it would seem,
fall into the ocean
with the most brilliant colors of pink and orange you could
imagine
a dream come true for a poet, or a sight da Vinci may have only
seen in his dreams, yet he doesn't write a word and he doesn't
feel a thing.
The next morning, he watches the sun rise over the mountains of
the main land and bounce off the cobblestone pathway into town,
he walks through a small village passing an elderly Greek
woman
perfectly content to sweep her taverna, he passes a Greek man
sitting side saddle on a donkey walking into town...
there are no 21st century sounds...
no cars,
no music,
no cell phones ringing
the only sounds that exist today are the waves crashing on the
rocks
and the bells attached to the saddle echoing out through the
mountains,
yet he doesn't write a word,
and he doesn't feel a thing.
Weeks pass and the sights grow numerous with wonder. From
the Parthenon to the temple of Poseidon,
from the riots and protests,
to the refugees flooding the alley ways.
From the fear, and excitement, of being so far from home; to the
feeling of being home so far from home. Yet, he doesn't write a
word, and he doesn't feel a thing.

What happens when a singer loses her voice?
What happens when a dancer loses his rhythm?
What happens when a poet loses his words?

Falling Flowers

Why can't I breathe
the same air I used to breathe?
Why am I constantly battling this feeling
that I'm half the man I used to be?

Why am I startled when the dead flower
falls from the wilted stem?
When should I just accept the fact
that I may end up being one of them?

Squire Notes

Oh, great king
how your presence ignites the fire
that burns within
how your battle scars map your journey
like the great quest for truth,
but you stand there unbowed
wavering only to yourself in times of solitude,
as battle tested as you may be
you know the war within rages on,
and holds the utmost significance.
The blood drips from your temple,
streaking past protruding hairs
like a stream through a forest
weaving its way down to your chin
finally free
falling into dust below
turning the dust to mud
from the blood of the king.
Your hands, good king, mighty in their grip,
yet trembling with each step,
knuckles bruised
caved in by the jaws of the enemy.
Fingers contorted, disfigured
to more of a claw like resemblance than a hand,
but my king still you hold fast to your sword
knowing full well the weight she carries,
but know better still the weight she gains
if placed on the ground.

My good king, why do you continue on this journey?
Blood-soaked,
wounded,
and left to fight
with an army of only one?
Have you not proven yourself to the masses?
Have you not bathed in riches?
Have you not felt the warmth of many a maid?
Have you not slept in golden palaces,
with sheets made of such silk
the child himself would be fit to be swaddled in?
My good king, can you not see that no armies oppose you?
No more enemies gather outside the walls of your kingdom sir.
Yet, there you stand.
Battered, but willing.
Broken, but whole.
Crushed, but determined.
Eager to fall, eager to rise,
and it appears with sword in hand
you are your only potential demise.
Ah, now it has become clear my good king
why you continue to march into the horizon's mystery,
you alone have the power
to build or burn
your own history.

Rosie

I said, "hey Rosie, what's your real name?"
She said, "my name's Danielle,
it's nice to meet you."
"It's nice to meet you as well.
Tell me your story;
tell me about your life."
"Well I dance on this pole
to put food on the table.
I have a little girl.
She's my world.
She's all I care about.
So, I let these guys feel up on me
and twirl my hair around,
but I got big dreams.
I wanna open up a restaurant
and serve up some Jamaican food.
You know, ox tail,
curried goat,
some fried plantains.
But, it's easy to let that drift working this job.
Sometimes I wanna go insane.
After I leave the champagne room
and I'm washing out my mouth,
I think about getting my daughter
and heading down south.
Just leaving this shit behind;
leave it in the rearview.
Set my sights on something beautiful,
something new.

I stare off into the distance when I'm here
but the distance is more glitter,
and another mirror.
Working for tips,
twerking for tips,
$20 a dance.
Trying to get a second glance
so I can take them up to the private room.
Try and seek out potential prey,
maybe a bachelor party,
lookin for the groom.
I just turn my brain off when I'm here.
I go somewhere else in my mind.
I don't even look at these dudes.
I just go blind.
All I think about is doing this for my baby girl.
I wanna give her all the things I didn't have;
I wanna give her the world.
But, right now, this is my only opportunity;
this is all I know,
all I'm good at.
This is the only thing keeping my baby girl
from growing up like a hood brat.
So, I strip.
I dance.
I take off my top.
I work the game
until I make em pop,
and they open their wallets,
and let some money drop
on the table.
I'm living in a fable.

I leave smelling like Jack D
or some combination of gin and tonic,
mixed with a little chronic,
and the ringing in my ears is sonic.
My head pounds.
I get headaches.
I had some luck on stage tonight,
had to bust out the rake.
Now I'm heading home
smelling like booze and sweat,
but it's hard to regret what I'm doin
when I see that little girl man.
I just wanna give her the world.
When I get home, I brush my teeth
and make sure I'm looking right
before I go in and see her,
and kiss her goodnight.
She's asleep in her room,
just dreaming, so sweet and peaceful.
That's why I do what I do.
That's why I work in this grease hole,
and work this greased pole.
I'll do whatever it takes
to keep this family whole.
I'll crawl to hell and back,
do my time,
and pay the toll.

Shit, I'd do anything,
I'd sell my soul.
Every night is a blur,
I'm serious.
Everything I do is for her,
period."

Recurring Dreams

Words and phrases spin in my mind
and call like a telephone
images and memories play in my mind
pull them out like weeds overgrown
I sit in the dark
alone in a room
but I'm in a crowded house
sprinting from door to door
the handles burn my hand and won't let me in
I'm trapped in the hall
and the memories continue to call and call
I pound on the doors
please let me in
please keep me safe
the floor starts to burn my feet
and I don't know this place
I don't know this home
I can't scream loud enough
the walls are six feet thick
the clocks blast with a tick tick
and a tock tock
I cock the gun
like a lock stock barrel and roll
continue to deal continue to fold
I'll play every hand cash all my chips
spin the roulette wheel and call when it flips
look when the river turns
fold on the flop
I'll keep betting until I take the pot

and I sit on my throne at the top
but the casino fades away
there goes the money
I'm sipping on smoke and vinegar
it used to be honey
gave me a little buzz
but when you're so high
you stay high
with watery eyes
you wave bye
with a bloody hand
till you can cauterize and stop the flow
stop the bleeding
my whole life I've been lying
I've been deceiving myself
I'm stuck in this castle searching for keys
looking for locks
I run and I run
inside this four-walled box
The walls turn to mirrors
and all I see
is me
for a thousand years
a thousand of me
a thousand bees
stinging my skin
stinging my soul
I try to overcome
circumstances
beyond my control
but no one will notice
if someone comes in
then I could show this

show them this hallway
show them this trap
see what they say
when I break the walls
break the mirrors
so I can no longer see
paint the walls black
paint the walls white
I can see for eternity
and no ones in sight
It's just me
It's just me
It's just me…

This Dance

Remember me,
And how we used to sleep
until noon?
Underneath the covers,
coming out when
we felt the moon?
But, we came to an end
so soon.
Sometimes it feels
like we didn't even start.
There was the beginning,
then the depart, which
is the hardest part for me.
At the end of the day,
we really weren't
anything.
But, it didn't feel that way
in the moment.
We slingshot into each other
like we reached back
and pulled it,
or a risky hand
but we decided not fold it.
We pushed all of our
chips into the middle.
But, I could never
figure you out
like a riddle.
You were gone even when

you were with me.
I know you might hear this
and disagree.
I just hope I never
caused you any misery.
I hope you look back
at us with better
memories.
But, if you don't
I just need you to remember
please.
That I was a scared little kid
what did I know?
I was acting like I knew,
but I put on a show for you.
I just wanted to make
you laugh.
I didn't see you showing up
in these paragraphs,
at least not in this
context.
I thought you would
make an appearance
in the proud sense,
like I couldn't believe
I got to see you every
morning,
but we always held back
like there was more
to the story.
Because our hearts were
running in different directions.
I think we both met at the same

intersection.
With the same thoughts of
this probably won't work out
but for now,
let's stick to this ill-fated route.
Find comfort in each other's
arms.
Even if in a little while we hear
the alarms,
and come back into reality.
But, I just need you to know
that it wasn't fake.
It was real to me.
And, I want to thank you
for helping me feel things.
Even if it was guilty,
or filthy like when the
cake was on the floor.
Remember that moment
when we both wanted to
close the door,
and forget about everyone
in the other room?
If I would have known it would
end so soon…
Maybe that's the moment
I would choose to go back to.
Oh, but, better yet it would be
the one in the classroom.
When you rubbed my back
and I read to you,
and I didn't know the words,
but I pretended to.

We could feel the tension
waiting to make the moves,
fighting with apprehension,
ignoring all the clues
because we knew it would be wrong.
But, wait! Don't leave.
Help me memorize one more song.
Are you hungry?
Because I could eat.
We'll sneak out the back
keep it low key.
Nobody will see us,
and if they do,
we'll hide behind these tree trunks.
We'll go wherever we need to go.
Just come with me, no one will know.
Let's go to our favorite place,
and see all the samples they
have to taste.
Then you can laugh at the look
on my face when
my favorite one gets
put away.
You've got to be kidding,
of all the days?
But, see, right there;
it's that laugh I miss,
and those lips
that I never got a chance
to kiss.
It was always hard
to look into your eyes
and realize this wouldn't last.

But, still, nonetheless
I didn't want time to pass.
I wanted to stick it out
until the end.
Even if we were just
playing pretend.
But, now, when we see
each other we always
share that look
of what could have been.
Maybe in the end
we were to each other,
all that we were meant
to be.
In both our moments
of feeling trapped
we made each other feel
free.
So, maybe you aren't meant
to be part of my destiny.
But, I'll still never forget
what you meant
to me.

Where It Clicked

Feel it in the air
rain falling down
acid rain falling down
full disclosure
maximum exposure
locked in a mental torture
painting a portrait of my soul
torn into pieces
pressed into creases
speaking fast
floating high
lyrical exercise
lyrical therapy
tie me to chair
then let me be
find my church
pray for rebirth
chipped yellow paint
signifies the line
what if I crossed it
what if I tossed it
my body in the way
remember the day
continue to pray for me
continue to say to me
that you love me
that you need me
tell me please
toss and turn like the seas
at night losing my sight

lost my vision
can't make a decision
can't process a thought
all my life is bought
purchased more and more
time scraping by
scraping my heart
against the pavement
the little boy screaming
the little boy crying
the lion rising
the little boy dying
words
dimes
rhymes
crimes
somethings gotta save you
dimes
crimes
rhymes
words
somethings gotta pay you
starving for air
starving for water
thirsting for direction
thirsting for distortion
a mind of epic proportion
can't deal
can't feel
can't tell you why
I see myself from a bird's eye
can you feel it for me?
Can you steer my heart for me?

Take the reigns
take the lights
turn them off and blind me
push me off the bridge
and find me
deep in the water
deep in the mind
of a twisted giant
twisted angel
walking through danger
thinking of something stranger
something dark
something heavy
feeling like a dead me
not real
no feeling
no peeling from the sun
cash my chips
check please
I'm done.
Shatter the mirror
kaleidoscope me
keep spinning and twisting
until you distort me.
Remember when I felt like a king?
Remember when I felt invincible?
Now every step I take I feel I'm dispensable.
Throw me out,
dispose of me.
Don't talk about it,
don't disclose on me.

Hide down deep
tuck it away,
catch your breath,
but breathe it in another day.

A Man on 30th AV

I'm down on my luck

I spent my last dollar

and just lost my shirt

I'm down to my last toss
I'm playing my last set
excuse me sir are you going to finish that cigarette?

I haven't been home for years
in fact I've forgotten where I'm from
there used to be a family that loved me
I even have a son I haven't met
excuse me sir are you going to finish that cigarette?

My stomachs rumbling
I haven't eaten for days
there's a cup at my feet with some change
but without 25 cents more there's no food I can get
excuse me sir are you going to finish that cigarette?

I'm sitting on my box
that's harvesting everything I own
my shoes are worn
and my pants have holes everywhere
that makes them look like a net
excuse me sir are you going to finish that cigarette?

Conversation doesn't come my way anymore
and the loneliness eats at my soul
no one by my side but a cockroach
so I'll keep him as a pet
excuse me sir are you going to finish that cigarette?

People walk by me like I'm a statue
they kick me away like a pigeon on the sidewalk
they look right past me as if I don't exist
but I'm not dead yet
excuse me sir are you going to finish that cigarette?

The Window's Reflection

What if the woman on the sidewalk
grew younger with each passing step?
Would she recognize herself
if the shoulders met,
forcing her eyes to lock?
Would she be pleased to meet her,
proud of who she became?
Would she turn away quickly,
to hide the shame
of a life lived through pain?
Running through the sunshine,
but always stopping to smell the rain.
Would she tell the young girl of pleasantries
she'll feel through the years?
Or, spill a haunting melody of
poison in her ear?
Would she warn her of future moments,
pain and loss?
Or, let her go about her day
knowing she, too, will learn
from carrying the cross.
Would she be surprised if she cried
while lost in her eyes,
so full of dreams?
Would she beg and plead for her
to hold on to those wonders
by any means?

Would she hold her;
never wanting to let her go?
Would she tell her all the notes
she ought to know?
Or, watch her life played back
as if seen through a picture show?
Would she let her walk by
remembering where she's off to?
Or, would she gasp through tears,
remembering what she'll go through?
Would she stand still
through a window's reflection,
appreciating this moment of
introspection?
Would she smile, because above all else
she knows of the beauty
time will bring,
and the wonderful song
her life will sing?

Dancing in Parking Lots

How long can we keep up this dance?
Is a lifetime too long to hold on,
just in case you change your mind and take a chance?
As much as I've tried to move on, my hearts gone.

See, I can see it right there in your eyes,
when you talk about him they don't light.
I know you're searching, telling little lies,
do you ever find yourself picturing me at night?

To be honest, I'm not sure I can stand this,
it's starting to break me apart again.
Don't you notice how perfectly your hand fits?
If only we could travel to way back when.

It's been years, but here we are at the coffee shop.
Still spinning in circles, still holding back.
The moment I see you I still feel my stomach drop;
I get butterflies every time, my mind gets off track.

I know you're in a place that's difficult to leave,
and there's a fear associated with us.
What if we don't become what we see in dreams?
What if it all proves to be pointless?

Is it possible for two souls connected
to not intertwine once they're set free?
Or, maybe these visions I've projected
will remain inside for only me to see.

But, what if we could be everything we dreamed?
What if our love isn't as far-fetched as it's always seemed?
Maybe we can run away to that island by the sea,
so that your breath is the only air I ever breathe.